KT-393-905

YOU & YOUR CHILD
SUCCESSFUL LEARNING

COPYRIGHT

Every effort has been made to trace copyright holders and to obtain
their permission for the use of copyright material. The authors and
publishers will gladly receive any information enabling them to rectify
any error or omission in subsequent editions.

First published 1999

Letts Educational
Aldine House
Aldine Place
London W12 8AW
Telephone 020 8740 2266

Text: © BPP (Letts Educational) Ltd 1999

Authors: Roy Blatchford and Tony Eaude
Series editor: Roy Blatchford
Project manager: Alex Edmonds
Editorial assistance: Tanya Solomons

Design and illustrations: © BPP (Letts Educational) Ltd 1999
Design by Peter Laws
Illustrations by Madeleine Hardy
Cover design by Peter Laws

All our Rights are Reserved. No part of this publication may be
reproduced, stored in a retrieval system, or transmitted, in any form or
by any means, electronic, mechanical, photocopying, recording or
otherwise, without the prior permission of Letts Educational.

British Library Cataloguing in Publication Data
A CIP record for this book is available at the British Library.

ISBN 185758 9815

Colour Reproduction by PDQ Repro Limited, Bungay, Suffolk.
Printed and bound in Italy

Letts Educational is the trading name of BPP (Letts Educational) Ltd

Letts Educational would like to thank all the parents who sent in their tips for educating children
and who wrote with such enthusiasm about parenthood.

YOU & YOUR CHILD
SUCCESSFUL
LEARNING

Roy Blatchford and Tony Eaude

Contents

Words in **bold** are defined in the glossary at the back of this book.

"Do not confine your children to your own learning for they were born in different time."

HEBREW PROVERB

Dear Parent,

What happens at nursery and in primary school is vital to your child's education. What you do at home is just as important.

It's never too soon to start supporting your child's learning. The time that you spend with your child in the first months and years gives him or her a foundation that lasts a lifetime. Make the most of every opportunity for you and your child to enjoy learning together.

You don't need to be an expert. You do need to be enthusiastic. Remember that the time you invest at home will help your child achieve all through primary and secondary school and open up opportunities for him or her in the future.

This book is one in a major new series from Letts. It will help you support your child, with information about building your child's self-confidence. It gives practical advice on extending school work into home learning. It also tells you how to develop your child's own particular abilities.

I hope you enjoy sharing successful learning with your child. The important thing is to make the experience fun!

ROY BLATCHFORD
Series Editor

What will help my child do well?

We all want our children to do well. Sometimes we aren't sure how we can help, or are so keen for our child to succeed that we put too much pressure on him or her. This book is a guide for parents to help them help their child become a successful learner.

Remember that children are individuals, with different aptitudes and abilities. They may inherit or learn some from you, but there will be many other sides to your child's character that you don't recognise. A successful learner needs to develop his or her own interests, in his or her own way.

Parent tip

"Encourage your child's enthusiasm and excitement for learning. Enthusiasm in one area is infectious and will increase your child's chances of success in all subjects."

The best way to help your child succeed is to encourage, support and extend his or her interests and knowledge.

Babies and young children are learning all the time. As he or she grows up, your child will naturally learn awareness of his or her own body, of other people, of self-control and of language.

Children do not learn exactly like adults. Young children learn in many different ways:

✔ by listening and imitating

✔ by copying from role models

✔ by experimenting

✔ by playing

Parent tip

"Always ask what 'special' thing your child has enjoyed each day."

Learning for young children is an active process. Look at any toddler to see how much he or she learns by doing things and exploring! Young children learn more by seeing and copying than through what they hear. This is obviously true for babies, but we forget that this is still true right up to adolescence.

Children are always coming across unfamiliar things and constantly testing out ideas against experience (things they have learnt). They are always asking questions – sometimes of themselves, sometimes out loud. Give children a wide range of different experiences as well as the chance to try them out for themselves and think, or talk, about what they have done.

Young children concentrate for shorter periods and move in and out of tasks much more freely than adults. They learn differently to adults. The divisions into specific subjects are nothing like as clear as for adults. So it's often hard to avoid imposing an adult's view of learning onto your child.

Don't think only of reading, writing, maths and other school subjects when looking at children's learning. These are important, of course, but the right attitude and approach to learning is far more important. Without this, your child will not be a successful learner.

What is a successful learner?

Successful learners almost always have the qualities mentioned below. Develop and encourage these qualities.

Your child won't become:

- ✔ independent......if you do everything for him or her

- ✔ confident.......if you criticise too much

- ✔ secure..........if you are inconsistent

- ✔ resilient........if you don't let him or her make mistakes

- ✔ reflective..........if you fuss around him or her too much

How should I try to support my child?

Be positive. Celebrate your child's interests and praise his or her successes. We all learn more from being told what we've done well than from negative criticism.

Parents are the most important teachers. Without love and care, children don't have the secure environment in which to feel safe and to take risks. We don't always get it right, but it is important to remember that how we behave teaches children a lot. Children learn from other children and grown-ups, especially about how to get on with other people. So find opportunities for your child to play with others, and to meet your adult friends.

> **Parent tip**
>
> "Read to your child from an early age. I showed my child books from the age of six weeks and at ten weeks she was playing with them. She has always loved being read to, especially at bedtime."

One useful idea is that of **surface learning** and **deep learning**. When we learn facts, we often forget them or can't transfer them to another context (use them in a different way). This learning is only on the surface. Deep learning occurs when we understand the patterns and thoughts behind those facts and when we can use our knowledge freely. To gain this takes time, thought, discussion and a wide range of different experiences. For example, if your child is interested in the leaves on the ground in autumn, talk and wonder together about other changes that happen – flowers dying, people growing taller, bread going stale, the weather getting colder, animals hibernating and so on. Don't overdo it, but try to help your child see the links and patterns rather than just the bare facts. Often you will find your child making links you had never thought of!

> **Parent tip**
>
> "I had the most loving parents ever, and that gave me such a feeling of security throughout life. I was determined to do the same for Peter."

Loving and caring for children is the most important thing of all.

If children are always too busy, they have no time to reflect and think about their experiences – on their own or with grown-ups. This is absolutely vital for children to make sense of themselves and their experience. Often – especially as children get older – what they need most is parents to be there, to be available and to pay attention to them. So don't overload your child's day with activities and organised events.

How can I learn more about supporting my child?

You can learn from a variety of people and sources:

✔ health visitors and doctors

✔ adults at nursery and playgroup

✔ teachers at school

✔ books, papers and the media

✔ other parents and other adults (including your own parents)

They will not know the particular needs of your child, so do not be blinded or confused by what everyone else says. But they will be able to offer advice and help put things into perspective.

How to help

No two children are the same. There is no one right way to support your child. Learn about your own child's needs by watching and learning. But aim to give:

✔ encouragement and praise – to give your child security and self-esteem

✔ high but realistic goals – to aim for further success

✔ time and opportunities to talk about what your child has done, or how he or she feels – to encourage thought and reflection

✔ clear boundaries – to be safe and to explore what is right and wrong

The most important things our children learn are about right and wrong and making choices. If we let them have everything they want, they won't learn about boundaries (limits). If we don't let them make their own choices, and mistakes, they will never learn for themselves.

Being a parent is probably the hardest but the most rewarding job in the world. Everyone makes mistakes, but loving and caring for children is the most important thing of all.

> ### Parent tip
>
> "Alan is an only child and we have always made extra efforts to make sure he has plenty of friends around him. Being with other children allows a child to gain a sense of who he or she is."

Is play important?

Young children are independent and successful learners. They learn a lot about themselves and the world around by play. For a toddler, building a tower with bricks is not just fun – it helps him or her understand about space, balance, height, friction and gravity. Talking to a doll and dressing it up teaches a child about other people and how to relate to them. Every aspect of play helps your child in some way.

> **Parent tip**
>
> "I think children learn through imaginative play, and also use it as a way to work out problems and concerns, such as a new baby coming, a death in the family or moving house."

CHILDREN LEARN MOST WHEN PLAY IS:

- ✔ active
- ✔ imaginative
- ✔ varied
- ✔ sustained for a period of time

Help your child play in a variety of ways in different situations. Don't always rush from one thing to another. You won't always succeed. Children, like grown-ups, need their independence and certainly won't willingly be pulled away from a game they are enjoying.

PLAY COMES IN ALL SHAPES AND SIZES! AT DIFFERENT TIMES, YOUR CHILD NEEDS TO PLAY:

✔ on his or her own

✔ with other children

✔ with adults

Your child won't always need expensive or sophisticated toys – though you will probably be under pressure to buy them at some time. Babies often like the wrapping paper more than the present! Your child may enjoy skipping or bouncing a ball, or playing with dolls or cars just as much as electronic games which cost a lot of money and may last only a few weeks.

Children learn how to get on with other people through play. Brothers and sisters can often do this well, but there may be a lot of rivalry. Once your child starts nursery or playgroup, encourage him or her to invite friends round or to visit other children's houses. The more people your child meets, the more experiences he or she will have to learn from.

Playing together

Remember to play with your child. Children need to play with different adults. If you are a single parent, try to find trusted relatives, especially of the other sex, to play and provide good role-models. Very often children have a close relationship with their grandparents.

Parent tip

"When my son was learning his times tables we used to practise by repeating them parrot-fashion in a relaxed environment (even in the bath!). When he was more confident I would fire random tables questions at him. He loved the challenge."

What should I play?

Children are much better at playing than adults, who often seem to have forgotten how to do it! Much of a child's play comes naturally, so look out for everyday situations – such as bathtime, going to the shops or in the park – where you are both relaxed and in different environments.

You will – usually! – both enjoy playing games together. At home, this could include:

- ✔   card games (such as Snap or Happy Families)

- ✔   board games (such as Snakes and Ladders)

- ✔   puzzles and toys

and when you go out

- ✔   ball games

- ✔   running games

- ✔   playing on swings, slides and other playground rides

But don't be too serious about what you are playing, or go on once children have got bored. Your child may want to play with you for a bit, then on his or her own or with other children. There is no value in forcing children to play! Remember that for young children play is the same as work, so don't impose the distinction between work and play too soon.

Above all, have fun playing alongside your child and talking about what you are doing

Should girls and boys play differently?

Boys and girls often play in different ways. Boys are often more boisterous and aggressive, and girls can be quieter and more social. Of course there are exceptions to this. This is probably partly natural and partly something that children can learn. You can't change it completely (even if you want to) but you can influence it.

Try to strike a balance between forcing your views on to your child and offering no direction. Help your child develop individual interests and ideas by providing a range of opportunities. Encourage some of the more unusual interests because otherwise peer pressure will probably draw him or her back to more conventional activities. Above all, let your child develop into his or her own person.

To avoid stereotyping, encourage girls to play with computers and construction toys, as well as dolls. And help boys to play calmly on their own and with other children, not just to charge around.

Parent tip

"My daughter goes to a gymnastics club after school. She enjoys mixing with her school friends while doing an activity that is not academic."

Often, when boys first go to school they don't know how to play with other children. So they copy other children – and it's often the 'wrong' bits of their behaviour! Learning how to make friends doesn't come naturally. It can be really helpful for children from the age of three upwards – especially boys – to talk about how to play with other children. Discuss what they did that made playtime more or less enjoyable – why they got into an argument or why they didn't share something.

No-one quite knows why many boys find it harder to make relationships. Reasons probably include:

- boys naturally mature later than girls

- boys are often more insecure emotionally

- adults usually expect and accept bad behaviour from boys

- group pressures from other boys

- stereotypical male behaviour on television

Encourage your child to play and make sure he or she knows how to play nicely

Having a good adult male role model certainly seems to help boys. And being very clear about what is acceptable in behaviour and how best to make friends seems to be more important for boys than girls.

Do nine- and ten-year-olds still need to play?

Yes! Though the way they play changes. This may be more social, through sports or organisations like the Brownies, or more individual, like spending more time with dolls or computer games. This is part of your child developing his or her personality. It may mean your child being passionate about one thing for several weeks or months and then losing all interest. Encourage a wide range of interests but make sure a hobby doesn't become an obsession. You may not be popular but you may have to ration the amount of time spent on something if your child really is spending all his or her spare time on this hobby.

What if play becomes too aggressive or rough?

Physical activity – climbing, swinging, running, and kicking in the playground, or the garden, or at the seaside – helps children to learn about themselves and their environment. Again, strike a balance between letting your child take sensible risks – which allow him or her to test boundaries and learn about the world – and not getting carried away with rough play. Play fighting frequently leads to real arguments, especially at school. If this happens too frequently, try asking your child what the game is called and how it is played. Games should have rules, and setting boundaries to rough play can help.

Quiet times are important too: times when your child can talk with you – or even just sit and think alone! Don't forget to enjoy a quiet snack or cuddle together. **Quality time** with a parent is vital for a child to become a successful learner.

How can I help my child's language development?

Learning to speak and listen is probably the most complicated skill any of us ever learn. Reading and writing come later, but they are built on a secure foundation of *spoken* language.

You will often see your child talking to him or herself during play. Children ask questions out loud and find answers as they play. Listen to a baby to hear how playing with sounds helps learning about language. They experiment with sounds and this helps them learn about language.

Very young children learn language at an amazing rate. And no one really knows quite how they do it. But it certainly helps them to:

✔ hear language spoken by adults

✔ imitate and try out sounds and words for themselves

✔ be corrected

✔ learn to correct themselves

This starts from the moment a baby comes into the world.

Language skills

As your child gets older, he or she will develop more sophisticated language skills by:

✔ asking and answering questions

✔ listening to, and speaking, language in many different situations

✔ exploring language alone

✔ learning formally about sentences and grammar at school.

If you have ever gone abroad and tried to learn another language, think about what helped you. Usually, this includes people speaking clearly, slowly and sympathetically. You also need to have the chance to try out new words and sentences for yourself in order to develop the language. But when people shout it usually isn't very helpful!

What if my child is learning English as an additional language?

All children need to learn English to do well at school. Those children who grow up in a home where English is not the first language have both a challenge and an advantage. When children have mastered one language well they can use those skills to help them learn another language. What is useful for children learning English as a first language is true for children who learn English as a second or third language too. But in addition:

> **Parent tip**
>
> "Gopal's teacher was great. She made him feel very special by praising his skills in Hindi, rather than stressing the fact that his English language skills were not as good."

• try to ensure that children learn their first language securely. Keep using it at home once your child goes to pre-school. Children who speak two or more languages have a great advantage and probably know more about language itself than other children. But unless your child learns the home language really well, difficulties are likely.

• recognise that children learning **English as an additional language** are likely to be behind with reading and writing in English in their first few years at school – but should catch up between the ages of seven and 11. This does not mean your child is stupid, simply less experienced. But schools can be unsympathetic. Help teachers to recognise your child's strengths both in language and elsewhere. Both home and school should have high expectations, but without expecting instant results.

Language skills

Language is the essential learning tool. We learn about colour or music, about the environment or ourselves, and many other things, by understanding and using the appropriate language. The foundations of maths start with counting the number of coins in your purse, or helping to lay the table or with the cooking. Your child will learn about science partly through observation and experiment, partly through naming and describing the world.

TIPS

✔ provide plenty of opportunities for talking and listening

✔ don't 'talk down' to children

✔ use interesting words to describe experiences

✔ have fun with long, or strange-sounding, words

✔ keep reading stories to children long after they have learnt to read for themselves

All children need to hear language spoken in proper sentences. Learning words is relatively easy, but working out how they fit together comes later, mainly by listening to and copying other people. Make sentences interesting by using:

✔ adjectives – such as 'enormous', 'shiny' or 'withered'
✔ adverbs – such as 'grimly', 'horizontally' or 'eternally'

Language is used in many different situations: around the house, going to the shops, visiting people, listening to the radio or story tapes, or watching television. Children need not just to hear language, but to use it and try it out for themselves. Provide plenty of opportunities for talking and listening. Songs and nursery rhymes help children's sense of language and rhythm, which is important in learning to read. Many children learn different uses of language through jokes, puns and riddles.

CHILDREN LOVE WORD-PLAY:

Jokes: "What is French and wobbly?"
　　　"The trifle tower!"
Puns: "When she planted her bulbs, all the flowers shone in the dark."
Riddles: "What has four legs in the morning, two at midday and three in the evening?"
　　　Answer: "A person – crawling when a baby, standing when a grown-up, walking with a stick when old."
Alliteration: "Silent spiders spin silky softness."

Is telling stories useful?

Telling and reading stories is both important and enjoyable. Children learn about how a story unfolds, how characters develop, using the voice to tell a story, and many other things from hearing stories. Many stories teach children about right and wrong and help them to cope with what they are afraid of.

> **Parent quote**
>
> "We used to put pop music on and get Imran and his sister to spot the first adjective or the first noun. It was chaotic but fun — and helpful to both of them."

Do boys and girls learn in the same way?

Boys have more problems than girls in acquiring language. They tend to start every stage – talking, reading, writing – later and often have more difficulties. This is partly to do with how the brain works, partly to do with behaviour and lack of concentration. More boys have reading difficulties than girls and they may become discouraged if they are not given extra help and support.

You may have to work harder to help boys' language development. And be more imaginative, for instance by using non-fiction and comics rather than just story books. But whether your child is a boy or a girl, the same rich diet of language and support is needed.

What can I do to help a child who has language difficulties?

Most children learn language skills well and without too much difficulty. For some, however, it is an uphill struggle or there is a definite problem. Watch out for any language delay or difficulty and don't be afraid to seek help. Early help from a speech therapist or other professional may make all the difference.

How can I help with reading and writing?

There is no one age when all children should be able to read. Reading is a skill we carry on learning right into adulthood. All children are different. Many start recognising words from the age of three, others not until after they start school.

HELP YOUR CHILD TO LEARN TO READ BY:

✔ having a range of books around, especially picture books

✔ pointing out words on notices, road signs etc.

✔ telling stories and reading books to and with your child

✔ reading books and magazines yourself to show that reading is a fun activity

Parent tips

"Try to find topics they are interested in. Each child is different and it's best not to force the issue if they are really not interested. Let them see you reading if you enjoy it."

"I try to read with my daughter every day. She loves it and it's a really pleasurable activity worth making time for. It reaps its own rewards."

ONCE YOUR CHILD STARTS SCHOOL:

Parent tips

"Read to your child from the earliest age possible. Read every night if you can, even if only for ten minutes. When your child can read alone, listen to him or her daily for at least five minutes. Encourage sign-reading when you're in the car or at the shops."

✔ show interest in, and read regularly, the books he or she brings home from school

✔ talk about the story and characters, why people acted as they did and what might happen next

✔ encourage your child to re-visit old favourites. Often reading a familiar book is a joy, whereas always struggling with what is hard can be frustrating and off-putting

✔ provide different types of reading material – magazines, comics, and non-fiction. For reluctant readers, especially boys, this sort of material often works better than stories

✔ remember that your child may learn at an uneven speed, at first in bursts, then more slowly

Establish a regular routine of a few minutes of quality time (when you give your full attention and the TV isn't on!) each day, or at least most days. But don't worry or feel guilty if you sometimes have to miss this.

How do we choose books?

Talk with your child about what he or she likes about a book. This may give clues to what types of books or authors your child likes. It can help if you suggest books. But don't do all the choosing – get your child involved in the choice!

Ask parents, librarians and teachers to recommend books they know children have enjoyed. Consider joining the local library and giving books for birthday presents. You can easily find cheaper books at charity shops, car boot sales and jumble sales, so the expense is not quite so great.

A word of warning

Reading is enjoyable, not a race. If a neighbour's child is on a higher level reading book, it doesn't mean that child is a better reader. Don't choose books which your child finds too hard. It is far better to enjoy and read a wide range of books at the right level than lose interest or confidence. There is a wealth of good material, so don't just choose school books.

What if my child finds reading hard?

Don't worry if your child is not reading at all by his or her fifth birthday. Keep checking for physical difficulties, with speech, sight or hearing, and talk to the teacher if you are worried. But, as a rule of thumb, be concerned if your child is still not making much progress recognising words and sounds by the time he or she is six.

When you read to pre-school children:

✔ enjoy the story for the sake of it, not just to teach reading, because children pick up on this

✔ point out rhymes and patterns in words

✔ let your child enjoy, and talk about, the pictures, not just the words

✔ get your child to turn the pages so that he or she feels in control

✔ don't go too quickly or you'll lose your child's interest

Read and tell stories at times associated with enjoyment, such as just after tea or in bed.

After a while, if you use your finger to point to the text you are reading, your child may start to join in with familiar phrases and recognise some words. Don't sound out words letter by letter. Use both letter–names and sounds when appropriate.

Parent quote

"Mark loves going to the library. I was surprised myself by how much more fun libraries are now."

Successful reading

You may know of the debate about whether children learn to read by **'phonics'** (sounding out words) or by a 'look and say'/'whole word' approach. The **Literacy Hour** emphasises phonics. All children learn to read by using both methods. Successful readers acquire the skills of each approach and choose which to use at what point.

How can I help my child with writing?

From an early age, encourage drawing and making patterns. Have lots of crayons, chalks, felt-tips and pencils available, as well as big sheets of paper. The drawings will at first be 'scribbles' but ask your child what they are about. Over time, they will be more recognisable. More importantly, your child is learning about hand-control and flowing movements – both of which are the first stages of learning to write.

Speaking comes before writing. Children must be able to say in their own head or out loud what they want to write. Often children forget what to write because they are concentrating so hard on letter formation. If need be, help your child to say what he or she wants to write – while you write it down. This is particularly important for children learning English as an additional language and those who find the physical act of writing difficult. A computer may help your child if he or she is full of ideas but cannot get them down quickly or neatly enough.

Left-handed writers

If your child is left-handed, make sure he or she:

- holds the pencil softly and doesn't change hands

- moves the pencil from left to right across the paper

- can see what he or she is writing – it's best to turn the paper at an angle

Children almost always become confident writers after they have learnt to read, though occasionally it happens the other way round. The reason is partly because **encoding** – making one's own messages – is harder than **decoding** – understanding someone else's messages; and partly because many young children have not yet acquired the co-ordination required for the physical act of writing.

Most children do not write recognisable words until they start at school. But many three- and four-year-olds write words, lists or labels, sometimes only the first letter is 'right' but gradually they learn about more of the sounds and letters and fit them together. This is often called **emergent writing**. Encourage this and point out what has been written correctly. Copying letters or words is only useful for practising hand-control. But hand-control is just what some children need.

How can I help with spelling?

Good readers are not automatically good spellers. Children tend not to 'pick it up' as easily as other skills. Successful spellers rely mainly on the look of words. Sounds help at the start of words and in the early stages of writing, so encourage this to start with. But help your child look at the shape of words, especially 'families' of similar words (such as *at, fat, sat, bat…*). Try to get your child to look at and write words as a whole, not letter by letter. Build on what your child does know, rather than give lists of unknown words.

IT HELPS YOUR CHILD TO WRITE:

✔ if he or she sits comfortably at a table on a chair of the right height, with his or her feet on the ground

✔ if he or she has enough space to spread out

✔ if he or she uses the non-writing hand to steady the page

✔ if he or she draws or writes with a soft pencil or crayon

✔ if he or she does not grip the pencil too hard

What happens when my child starts playgroup or nursery?

Starting at playgroup or nursery is a big step – both for you and your child. Until then, home has been the main focus of attention.

How can I help my child get ready to start?

Most children enjoy the chance to make new friends, but for most of us a change can feel scary or risky. Most nurseries or playgroups offer parents and children the chance to go and meet the teacher in advance. Do go if you possibly can. Be prepared to ask questions. And let them know about your child's particular (and real!) needs.

Finding out about the rules and expectations is important. For instance, what do children need to take? Is there a uniform or dress code? What are the arrangements for eating or snacks? Where do children hang their coats?

You can avoid a lot of worry or unhappiness simply by careful attention to detail. If your child struggles with shoelaces, velcro fastenings can make life much easier. If your child gets hungry, a little snack may be appropriate. Most importantly, listen to your child's questions and try to find out if he or she has any worries or fears.

What about daily routines?

Many parents lead very busy lives, fitting in a lot of commitments. Your own personal organisation and routines matter. If you are always in a rush, or late, that rebounds on the child. If you never have time for your children, you won't enjoy, or help, them as much as you could. Your child needs the chance to:

✔ talk about what is about to happen and what has happened

✔ organise his or her own time and space

✔ learn to do things independently

Learning can be messy – involving clay and paint and water – so don't send your child to playgroup or nursery dressed up for a party!

One of the really good things about pre-school is the opportunity to make new friends. You may find that your child gets invited to someone else's house – or wants to have a new friend back. Try to encourage this. It is all part of learning more about a wider circle of people – and is good fun!

These points may sound as if they have nothing to do with learning. But if children are worried and unhappy this will affect their progress. Watch out for signs of your child being unsettled.

Set aside quality time – a little and often – for your child as an individual. This can be really hard if you have several children who demand your attention or if you work full time. But try to find a regular time for each parent to spend with each child. Remember that, if possible, your child will benefit from both mum's and dad's attention. You will enjoy it and your child will benefit if you share out these special times.

Once your child starts, it is important that you:

✔ show interest in your child's day. Don't interrogate him or her on every aspect of the day, but do ask. Try to ask questions that require a specific answer (an answer in words), rather than just 'Yes' or 'No'. This may help if your child seems unwilling to talk.

✔ praise and encourage your child. He or she will probably bring home paintings or models. Put them up, label them, say 'Well done!'. When your child says how he or she has made a new friend, or counted to five, or made up a tune, show you are pleased.

✔ listen out for any problems or worries. What may seem trivial to you may cause real distress to your child. Young children feel emotions more intensely than adults.

How much should I 'push' my child?

You may be impatient for your child to get on quickly to 'real learning' – reading and writing and sums. Pushing children too hard into 'formal teaching' does not help them. Competition at this age is less important than later on. Pay attention to the questions your child asks. You will be amazed at his or her speed and ability to pick up new ideas. In the Early Years, in nursery and Reception classes, most learning comes through play. Concentrate more on:

✔ helping your child to co-operate with other children

✔ following your child's lines of interest

✔ suggesting new activities or ideas – especially if they are ones that build on what your child has just learnt

Try not to be over-protective. Children need to learn to sort problems out for themselves. They may need a helping hand, but parents who interfere all the time do their children no favours.

> ### Parent quote
>
> "I feel competition is healthy, as long as the methods are fair and there's no cheating. It builds up a sense of achievement, and can lead to a greater determination to do well at school."
>
> ### Parent tip
>
> "Children aren't usually good at everything – but everyone has something they can do well. Above all, praise them!"

This sounds like a long list of dos and don'ts. Try not to worry. You won't get it right all the time; you will make mistakes. But that's part of being a parent. Give your child a good secure start and the odds are he or she will go on to do really well.

Quality time

Walking to and from home may not be possible. But if you can, this can help your child by:

✔ talking about what is going on at nursery or playgroup

✔ discussing and taking different routes

✔ noticing what is going on, like road signs, changes through the seasons or familiar people

These are the foundations of subjects like reading and geography, and a chance to instil good habits like road safety and punctuality!

> ### THINK ABOUT:
>
> ✔ how do we travel to nursery or playgroup?
>
> ✔ who does the dropping off and the picking up?
>
> ✔ what is our daily routine?
>
> These things need to be considered because it is details like this that matter to a child.

Establish good routines for you and for your child.

How can I help my child make the mos of changes at school?

We all feel nervous and have mixed feelings about approaching changes – looking forward to new challenges and feeling worried about not being able to cope.

Much of the Chapter Five is also relevant when your child starts at infant or primary school. It is a big step, often from a fairly small, informal place where everyone is on first name terms to a more formal, larger place. For many parents, it is the time when your baby has become independent and doesn't need you so much!

Think and talk with your child about hopes and worries. Often other children, maybe older brothers and sisters, or older friends from nursery or playgroup, can help children both in advance and in the first few days by talking to them about what they are worried about. Parents of other children can help *you*. Remember that it's natural to worry about your child's first days at school.

Different schools have various ways of making the transition easier. Most invite parents to the school in the term before children start. Make sure you visit and get the prospectus, partly to get the feel of the place, partly to prepare for practical details about the school day and what your child needs.

Starting school

All children are different. Some take to school like a duck to water, others find it quite a daunting experience. When your child starts:

✔ try to build a routine of leaving the house, being on time and having everything your child needs (with your child being as responsible as possible for this)

✔ continue to find time to show interest. Ask about school. You may not get very full answers – but it is worth persisting! If you don't pick your child up, talk briefly with whoever does. And look in your child's bag and lunchbox (if he or she has one). You can find all sorts of important information – from letters to uneaten food!

Parent quote

"My husband was more nervous about Eve starting school than she was!"

Get to know the teacher, if you can, without being too 'pushy'. Often a few words at the start or end of the day will tell you a lot. Remember to say what has gone well, not just to complain! And make sure you go along to parent/teacher discussions.

What should I do about bullying?

This can be really hard for children, especially when they have just started school. It is a big and worrying environment where the rules – both official and informal ones – are often unclear. Many young children copy older children and get into bad habits or situations they can't really cope with. This is especially true for many boys who are not so skilled at social interaction. You may need to talk through how to make friends and to encourage particular games or friendships. If you are worried about **bullying**, go and discuss it with the teacher.

Listen and talk to your child about his or her hopes and worries.

Watch out especially for:

✔ tiredness, and with it unusually bad behaviour

✔ worries about friends and playtime

What about when my child moves class?

Children get very attached to their teacher and may worry about moving on to a new class. Children – and parents – can get very agitated. Children are taught by a range of adults with different approaches and interests over the years. You are bound to hear talk of the teachers who are really good, or the ones to avoid. Of course, some teachers are better than others at certain things, but most have different skills which may bring out a particular interest – and leave other aspects not so well developed, for now. The **National Curriculum**, and better curriculum planning, means that it is now unlikely your child will miss out on particular subjects or topics because of one particular teacher.

> **Don't forget...**
>
> • introduce yourself to the teacher
>
> • stay interested in your child especially when he or she does not seem eager to talk
>
> • be ready to spend time with your child even when you are busy

Moving class can affect friendships and classroom dynamics. Though it is good for young children to have at least one friend in a new class, part of growing up is extending that range of friends and teachers. Children are more adaptable than we sometimes think. Often, within a few weeks the new teacher has taken the place of the previous one as 'the best teacher in the world' and an old friend is forgotten in favour of a new one.

Children from the age of eight or nine are more reluctant for parents to be involved in what happens at school. This is natural and continues into the teenage years. Carry on showing an interest, even when it is not returned. Children need to know you are on their side, even if they don't show it, and will appreciate your concern, even if they don't say so.

Changing school

Children move schools at different ages, depending on where they live. But for most the big change is at the age of 11 when they go on to secondary school. This is a big step, but myths grow up about what might happen. Don't listen to everything you hear, and talk through possible worries with your child. Usually an open evening about six months before helps to highlight areas of concern, and visits in the term before can help to ease some worries especially on everyday things such as where the classroom is or what the teacher looks like.

Many children move school mid-year because of parental separation, moving house or other reasons. Settling in a new school takes a while. If this is the case, your child will need the chance to go over all the issues covered in this chapter again. Don't forget that he or she is also coping with the changes which caused the move. Be prepared to spend a lot of time with your child, at a time when you are probably busier than usual!

What are study skills?

Study skills relate to all aspects of life, not just schoolwork. They help your child become:

- ✔ independent

- ✔ determined

- ✔ questioning

- ✔ confident

- ✔ thoughtful

> **Parent tip**
>
> "Organisation of work, neatness – in writing and general layout – and an ability to understand a variety of information sources are all important study skills."

Your child will have begun to develop these at home, for instance, when he or she is learning to dress and, after amusing and exhausting efforts, at last succeeds in putting on a vest or pair of pants. Your child has persevered and shown him or herself to be confident and independent.

Learning to sit correctly at a table, hold a pen correctly, turn pages without tearing them – these are all basic study skills necessary for your child to succeed. Primary school is a time to concentrate on them and improve them.

If your child has physical difficulties, talk with your child's teacher or doctor. Referral to specialist help may be needed. Do this early in your child's school life – if conditions like glue ear or hand-eye co-ordination problems are not identified early, your child will suffer and his or her education will suffer too.

How do children learn?

We each have individual ways of learning. But remember certain key points about how young children learn:

CHILDREN'S CONCENTRATION IS LIMITED

Most children cannot concentrate for long periods of time. Adults find this hard enough, but expecting your child to sit for two hours without a break is a recipe for disaster! Make your child take regular breaks. Children learn best by sitting and applying themselves to the task set in short sessions – without being distracted. Use an alarm clock to time work sessions when your child is older. Perhaps even offer modest rewards, such as a favourite meal or sweet, at the end of a study session.

CHILDREN WILL LEARN BEST WHEN RELAXED

This does not mean lying on the floor with headphones on! But your child needs to be wide awake, not distracted by a TV screen or an inquisitive toddler. Learning requires the right materials and setting. In a good classroom children can do a task and enjoy their work, led and guided by the teacher. At home, you are that guiding influence. Support your child by helping when asked – and making time to talk through what the task is.

'WHAT'S IN IT FOR THEM?'

This is not about rewarding every good exam result with a new bike or computer game – though sensible rewards have their place. Your child needs tasks and targets that are achievable within a reasonable time. Learning and studying sometimes means success takes quite a time to come. That's when the extra bit of parental support over homework is vital.

> ### Parent quote
>
> "If I want him to concentrate at home, I make sure that we are quiet, no TV or music, sitting comfortably and then aim for short spells of concentration."

If you find your child is struggling – and perhaps tearful – have a break and return to the task later, rather than causing unnecessary upset. We all get blocked or frustrated sometimes. If this happens over a period of time, then talk to the teacher about the level of work your child is being given.

Parent quote

"You can tell if Stevie is struggling with work. He just shuts off. We always tell him to have a break and then he can try again when he's relaxed a bit."

CHILDREN LEARN IN DIFFERENT WAYS, USING ALL THEIR SENSES

We all have different kinds of intelligence. Some children may learn easily through talking and listening, while others learn better when they can use their hands. Young children learn more by seeing and doing than by hearing.

Good teachers and well-planned classrooms allow for children working with different approaches and at different speeds. But the National Curriculum sets out certain facts and skills that all children must learn. And teachers have to plan for a whole class. So your child may well face tasks which could be learnt more successfully in other ways – if you can make the time to do this at home, your child will reap the rewards.

When you support your child at home, remember that music, rhythm, role play, games and the computer screen can all be used as well as paper and pencil.

SURFACE LEARNING TO DEEP LEARNING

Much of what happens in school is about learning something one day, memorising and practising it, then using that knowledge or skill again the next day or the next week. As with adults, children transfer knowledge from short term to long-term memory, from surface to deep learning, by going back over what they have learnt.

Helping your child at home may therefore involve revising something that has been done at school – in a fun and memorable way! Words and music can help your child prepare for a test. Don't underestimate the use of visual clues to help children remember their spellings or times tables.

What particular study skills do older primary children need?

Study skills develop throughout life. Extra work on spelling or tables matters, but it is more important for your child to approach tasks independently. From eight or nine years old onwards, help your child to focus more on study skills – as more homework is expected.

Remember the old saying :'Give someone a fish and you've fed them for a day. Teach them to fish and you've fed them for life.' Don't give in to the temptation to over-protect your child during the school years. The more your child learns for him or herself, the better prepared he or she will be for the future.

Parent tip

"Independent research is an invaluable skill: looking things up in reference books or on the computer; learning to be selective; picking out the most important facts; learning to answer the question."

How can I help?

The best answer is: by doing more than the minimum. Teachers often set a task for homework that the child 'completes' in 20 minutes. If you spend ten minutes talking around the task set, you can probably suggest how your child can improve the answer by reshaping or developing a particular aspect. This is true of written or practical tasks.

Help your child to develop the art of researching. This is very difficult. Many university researchers spend years trying to find out just how best to do it! Suggest to your child that copying (or paraphrasing) from just one text is not enough. It's better to look at a number of sources and then put things in your own words. You can give valuable support here by using CD-ROMs and the Internet as well as dictionaries and encyclopaedias. Other sources of useful information are:

- newspapers
- magazines
- libraries
- television and radio programmes
- videos
- museums and exhibitions.

> **Important words and phrases**
>
> Without an understanding of the following 'command words' your child will not be able to understand what the tasks set at school mean:
>
> - why
> - how
> - where
> - give reasons for...
> - explain in your own words

Exam preparation is now a necessary study skill. The **National Tests** at ages seven, 11 and 14 are now very much part of school life. Teachers prepare children thoroughly for these. Find out from the school how this is done. Schools will often run information evenings on the subject. You can then back up your child's school learning with practice at home.

For your part, you can borrow or buy a range of practice test papers. It's a good idea to look through the test papers together to see how they are set out, what key words they use, what time is allowed for which questions, how many marks are given and so on.

Remember to get your child to test you, as well as the other way around!

Tips for parents

✔ Support your child with your *time*, not just in the primary years but throughout school life.

✔ Encourage reading, writing and number skills at home – don't leave school to do everything!

✔ Help your child feel positive about learning and gathering knowledge in general – and about going to school in particular.

✔ Support your child as he or she tackles any new skills – a child needs to feel that learning a new skill is an opportunity not a threat.

✔ Listen to and talk with your child about his or her interests and experiences.

✔ Emphasise that learning is fun – this is important for boys and girls alike, especially when friends want to dismiss school as 'boring'!

✔ Approach study skills as a shared piece of learning – allow your child to get ahead of you and show you a trick or two!

How to overcome common learning problems

How can I help my child to concentrate?

Some children, especially boys, find it hard to settle down to anything for a sustained period. Sometimes they will sit and play computer games for hours, but won't do anything involving other people.

Spend time regularly with your child. Hours alone with a computer or in front of the TV do not help children to concentrate on other things. Routines like regular mealtimes can help. Make sure your child gets enough sleep. Often children who are grumpy or unco-operative are tired. If physical patterns persist, such as broken sleep or nightmares, discuss them with your GP.

Many people think that diet influences children's behaviour. And there is a lot of discussion about **attention deficit and hyperactivity disorder (ADHD)** – a medical condition, diagnosed by a doctor, which means children cannot concentrate. Disorders like these exist but are not all that common. Most children who find it hard to concentrate need a lot of adult attention, a different level and type of stimulus (maybe more, maybe less) and, above all, clear boundaries and expectations.

Coping with problems

Difficulties are bound to occur. Try to help your child be resilient enough to cope with minor incidents which are part of growing up. Check constantly whether to get involved, but only intervene when necessary. If in doubt, remember:

✔ give most problems time to sort themselves out

✔ if you are really worried, don't be afraid to act

Parent quote

"My son finds it hard to concentrate if there is anything else happening around him. At home he has a desk in his room now and can concentrate more, but I found at a younger age he needed so much help that he had to work downstairs where I was."

What if my child won't do homework?

This depends very much on your child's age. Up to the age of eight or nine, most homework will not take a long time to complete, and can often be done with an adult. Older children may get more homework and be required to work independently.

Getting into a routine early on helps, for example reading with your five-year-old straight after tea, or for half an hour before bedtime. This makes it easier when children are older. Children need to develop the discipline of good study habits for secondary school.

Homework problems

If your child is finding homework difficult, try:

✔ working alongside him or her for a while

✔ talking through what to do and discussing problems

✔ checking to see if there is too much homework or it is too hard

If the homework seems unreasonable, talk to your child's teacher.

Parent tips and quotes

"I try to praise my son a lot at home if he does some writing or a good drawing, and I say I hope he concentrates that well at school."

"First of all, make sure there's nothing medically wrong, then find something he or she is happy doing and slowly encourage him or her to concentrate on it, one minute longer each day."

"However small the step, this is a giant leap forward and should not be compared with brighter or poorer performances of other pupils."

My child has got 'stuck'. What should I do?

It is very common for children to get 'stuck' with their learning, usually between the ages of seven and 11, but sometimes later. After a time of rapid progress, especially in reading, they may slow down, or say they are bored. We all learn at different rates, not always steadily, and slow patches can occur. Do share concerns with your child's other parent or with the teacher if this pattern continues for more than a few weeks.

Your child may be reluctant to talk about what is the matter; or may deny that there is anything wrong. Don't force the issue too much, but be there to listen, and follow up any worries that crop up. The problem may be a broken friendship or an unsympathetic teacher, or a worry about keeping up with the rest of the class. Or it may be more serious, in which case you may need to seek professional help.

Parent quote

"It took us ages to work out why Tim was so withdrawn and unhappy. It turned out that he was really worried about how he'd get to his new school."

My child is a good reader, but not very keen on reading

Try to carry on reading to, and with, your child until well after he or she has become an independent reader. Once children have become fairly independent readers, they sometimes reach a plateau and lose interest in books. Choosing books can be a real problem. Many children try to read very hard books and get bored with them. Sometimes just a change, for example to non-fiction, adventure stories or science fiction, can do the trick. Find ways to get the pleasure back into reading, even if the book is less challenging.

My child is not motivated by his teachers

Be careful. Often children say they are bored, when what they really mean is they aren't enjoying school but can't explain why. Sometimes children, especially able children, do find their school work too easy, or dull. Find out from the teacher what your child is actually doing at school. Offer help rather than criticism. The teacher may try a different approach, or you may be able to help: with projects, doing research at the library, using computers or practical problem-solving. More of what makes your child bored is unlikely to be much use. The trick is to strike a balance between providing new and interesting challenges, and encouraging your child to knuckle down to hard graft.

Tips for parents

✔ try not to fuss over minor incidents

✔ be there to listen to, and follow up, worries

✔ make sure children get enough sleep

✔ get into a homework routine from early on

My child is worried about moving to secondary school

Children often worry about moving schools. Becoming a small fish in a big pond is quite daunting. Exaggerated stories may cause real fears. Talk in advance with your child about hopes and worries, including details like where the toilets are and where children can change their clothes or what time lunch is served. Arrange for a visit on an open day or with the primary school. Often children find the uncertainty hardest to cope with. Seeing the school and the opportunities on offer really helps.

Primary teachers nearly always pass on information about your child's strengths and weaknesses to secondary schools. And usually teachers meet to discuss potential difficulties. If your child has special needs, especially physical disabilities, or is emotionally vulnerable, it may well be worth contacting the secondary school before your child starts. Keep an eye out for how your child settles in during the important first few weeks.

Remember that your child's 'unique' problem has usually been experienced by lots of other children. Talk to friends, to the teacher or to someone you trust to get things in perspective.

Coping with other problems

You probably see some parents and think they never have any problems. Not so! Being a parent is difficult. Not only is it a full-time commitment, but children change as they grow older and they often become harder to manage.

What about when my child just won't do what I say?

You're bound to meet this, whatever your child's age! It's part of being a parent. You will have to sort out your own response, but try to work out some principles – parents should do this together, if possible. Consistency is very important. Children need boundaries – they need to know that when you say no you mean no. But beware – children are very good at manipulating adults and playing parents off against each other!

Rewards and praise for good behaviour tend to work better than punishing bad behaviour, but sometimes you need to use punishment. Make punishment brief but fair, and avoid humiliating children, especially in public.

Knowing when to be there

As your child gets older, he or she may not want to let you help. Try to:

✔ give your child space

✔ be there when your child needs you

Smacking

Most parents try not to smack children. If you do, only smack your child straight away to show the danger or seriousness of what they have done. Don't do it because you have had a hard day or store it up for later.

Children have a very keen sense of justice and recognise when they have done wrong, but will feel aggrieved when the punishment is too harsh.

What if my child is more interested in what other children of the same age think than what I do?

Parent quote

"It was really hard not to get irritated when Laura seemed obsessed by her new best friend, Helen. It seemed as if she had no mind of her own during that period. Whatever Helen did was great!"

As children get older they become less interested in their immediate family, and more concerned with what their friends think and do. The particular make of clothes or toys really matters even to a seven-year-old. Many children can be genuinely unhappy if they feel left out of the group. There is no easy answer. You can't just buy whatever is in fashion – especially when it may only be used for a few weeks. Never buying what is in vogue will probably make your child's life hard, and yours even worse! Use occasions like Christmas and birthdays for presents or new clothes. But also learn to say no – and take the consequences. At times, of course, a special treat is fine but don't give in regularly to constant nagging.

What if my child doesn't want to go to school?

You are responsible for getting your child to school unless there is a good reason not to go. So you need to insist. It can be difficult if your child is very upset.

If your child is just a bit reluctant, give reassurance that you, or whoever, will be there to collect him or her at the end of school, mentioning something to look forward to after school. Occasionally it may be worth promising a treat – but be careful it doesn't become a pattern.

Be concerned if your child is constantly getting little illnesses – especially if he or she immediately gets better at home. It may be a sign of anxiety – about bullying or work worries, for instance. If this is the case, you should talk to the teacher. In more serious cases, talk with the school and, if need be, get professional help. A pattern of continued poor attendance can be much harder to resolve when your child is older.

> **Parent quote**
>
> "Tessa was always so keen to get to school, but then she started to complain of constant sore throats and was having a lot of time off school. It turned out that she'd fallen out with a group of girls who were making her life hell and she just couldn't bear to go to school."

Children involved in drugs or crime

Any child can get caught up in drugs or crime. Watch out when your child becomes more independent – from the age of seven or eight onwards – and spends more time on his or her own.

Some children get into trouble younger than adults imagine, sometimes in the older primary years. Often it starts with experiments and pranks, but leads to nothing. Don't be too dictatorial, but keep an eye out for changes in your child's behaviour, such as if he or she has unexplained sums of money, becomes secretive or acts very much out of character.

Try not to worry about it too much. Know where your child is and roughly what he or she is doing. This is partly for his or her own safety (and your peace of mind), and partly because children in groups sometimes get into trouble when they are quite young.

Talk about difficult issues – don't pretend they don't exist. And remember, however much you want to, it isn't in your child's best interests for you to be overprotective. Be aware and be available.

What if my child is being bullied or is a bully?

Your child may get bullied or may be a bully him or herself. Bullying is different from arguments or fights. It includes name calling (often about family, race or looks), teasing, ganging up or hurting other children. Bullying can affect boys and girls of all ages. It can lead to serious unhappiness, problems with learning and even crime.

If bullying is serious, or goes on for a long time, don't be afraid to go and talk to the school.

Parent quote

"We felt terrible when we found out that George was being bullied. It had gone on for months and we just hadn't noticed the signs."

Don't ignore bullying

Help your child to be independent and assertive.

✔ encourage your child to talk about problems

✔ ask about school worries, without interrogating your child

Discuss with your child what to do. And repeat it, or write it down. Tips might include:

✔ ignoring taunts for a while, especially if your child is easily provoked

✔ saying 'Stop it! I don't like being called names'

✔ walking away with a friend

✔ playing with other people, especially at playtimes, to avoid the bullies

✔ telling a 'dinner lady' or a teacher and, importantly, someone else if that doesn't work

Bringing up children is a serious matter, but it is also tremendously fulfilling. Above all have fun – enjoy your children and remember there are other people to help, not just professionals, but relatives, friends and neighbours.

What if my child has special abilities?

Children show their special abilities at different stages. It seems as if some children are different from others from a very young age. For other children, special abilities may not be obvious until well into primary school.

Look out for and respond to those interests and abilities. If your four-year-old develops an interest in Roman Britain, you may find yourself borrowing books from the library each week or visiting museums at the weekend. Another family may respond to a child's pet subject by buying Thomas the Tank Engine books and magazines, and visiting the local steam railway sheds.

Parent quote

"My eight-year-old daughter has a higher 'reading age' and I have found it hard to find appropriately challenging books which I feel are right for her level of maturity and not over-long for her concentration span."

How do I know if my child has a particular special ability?

Parent quote

"I don't think my daughter concentrates if she's bored – and she gets bored very easily. I wish 'special needs' extended to both ends of ability."

BABIES

Most babies watch, reach out and attempt new feats all the time. They respond to noises, colours and patterns. They enjoy learning – and learning is all about exploring. But some babies seem to be particularly enquiring and can become very frustrated by not being able to take the next step. They strive very quickly to sit up, then crawl, then walk. They may also be very demanding of your time.

These babies master skills very quickly. You need to balance the exploration, play and fun with periods of cuddles and quiet. We all need the quiet moments!

For many young children the first signs of special ability are early speech. Some children learn to speak as young as 11 or 12 months and may move quickly to speaking in full sentences and using correct grammar. You may be surprised one day to hear your child ask, 'Please may I have a biscuit?' when other children at playgroup are just pointing or using single words.

This stage can be difficult for parents. The child will enjoy the attention from adults, but parents don't want to be seen to 'show off'. As a parent, support – rather than push – this skill with language.

NURSERY

By nursery age some children do stand out from others. This may be because of:

✔ the rich variety of language they use

✔ their ability to count easily

✔ good general knowledge

Whatever your child's interest, try not to make your child feel that interest is wrong or that it makes him or her superior to other children.

Some able children find that at nursery their ability is a barrier to play. They may want to play games with rules too complex for others to follow. Sensitive handling by adults is important here, perhaps by joining in the play to keep it enjoyable for everyone.

> ### Parent quote
>
> "Ben's oldest brother used to really tease him about the fact that he loved maths and numbers. We really had to convince Ben that it didn't matter what Greg thought."

PRIMARY SCHOOL

Formal schooling is a time of great excitement for some able children and a disappointment for others. Do not be anxious if your child does not like school at once. Give your child time to settle. It is not realistic to expect that all schooling will be well matched to the needs of your child. There *will* be times when he or she is either bored or over-challenged.

Try to support your child in school by helping him or her think about what he or she is learning and to relate it to other things. Most able children learn skills quickly and do not need extra practice at home. You can talk to them about what they are learning and what they think about it. Assist them in school interests and follow up on things they are doing by visits to the library or looking up information on the computer.

As children move through primary school even those who are good at most things tend to show particular strengths. Watch out for two issues:

A word of warning

A handful of children seem to excel at everything they try. Here it is important to make sure that they do not become too busy – or over-pressed by parents.

- Some children begin to focus very strongly on areas that they find easy and do not want to take part in things where they do not excel. Encourage your child to develop a range of interests and help him or her to understand that he or she does not have to excel at things in order to enjoy them. A very musical child, for example, may not be especially good with technology – but he or she can still enjoy it.

- Most able children can do their school work without undue effort. This can mean that they become unused to working hard. If this occurs you need to talk to the teacher without delay. A good primary teacher will welcome knowing sooner rather than later if an able child is not being challenged in class. Learning to work and strive when things are difficult is important, and can be something that able children miss out on.

Challenge and support

Being a parent of an able child has its ups and downs, much like any other kind of parenting. It requires you to give love, be strong and nurture him or her tenderly.

The best way to support children is to value what they have and to help them to tackle things that they find difficult. This is not easy with any child. With able children it is tempting either to expect too much and therefore create pressure, or to see the child always in relation to his or her ability.

What about extra-curricular activities?

Learning is about more than just the subjects we learn at school. Many children's and teachers' best memories relate to **extra-curricular activities**. By these we mean experiences not part of the normal school curriculum, such as:

- ✔ art, drama, music and other creative opportunities

- ✔ sports – both team games and individual activities such as swimming

- ✔ clubs and groups like Cubs, Brownies and Woodcraft Folk

- ✔ visits to places, for example museums, libraries and the theatre

- ✔ residential trips to other parts of the country or abroad

Parent quote

"Both my children attended gym clubs – confidence in their success was the reward."

Serious fun

For some children who are very talented these activities can be the route to serious training and competition, such as in swimming or music. But for most children they provide chances for fun, for taking part and for learning different skills and approaches.

Children gain a great deal from these activities. They help to:

- ✔ build confidence, independence and self-esteem

- ✔ make new friends

- ✔ extend personal interests

Do all schools offer after-school care or play schemes?

More schools are now starting these, mainly designed for working parents. You may have to pay. They offer a chance for children to enjoy a range of activities in school where the emphasis is less on work, and more on free choice. Look out for:

✔ an emphasis on play and relaxation

✔ a safe, well-ordered atmosphere

✔ a wide range of activities, both quiet and energetic

> **Parent quote**
>
> "My daughter attends an after-school club. It's beneficial because she socialises with children other than those in her class."

What else could my child do out of school?

Many extra-curricular activities are arranged by schools, or by local organisations – or you could arrange them yourself. Going to a museum, a castle, the theatre or the seaside is great fun and helps children's learning. Trips such as these could be used to follow up a school project.

Long school holidays can be boring for children. Many local organisations arrange activities such as music workshops, sport tuition and drama groups. These can be great fun for children from the age of seven upwards.

Extra-curricular clubs are particularly good for many children who are shy or have special educational needs. Those who find school work difficult can often shine in a different environment, and even those who aren't 'the best' still get great enjoyment from other activities. But they may need you to encourage them a bit more than those children who are very confident. A lot of children take part in extra-curricular activities because their friends go. That's fine. But it often means that children who want to do unusual or unconventional things are put off because their friends don't go – or because they get laughed at. You may need to encourage your son to keep singing in a choir, or to go dancing, and your daughter to stick at football or playing the trumpet.

Parent quote

"My children attended several different after-school clubs. Their social skills and confidence improved; their awareness developed, and at Scouts useful badgework helped with schoolwork and independence and discipline resulted."

A teacher writes

When I taught in one primary school, I used to run a chess club for half an hour each week. It attracted all sorts – the very serious, the ones who never really learnt the moves, boys and girls who liked a chance to play quietly with their friends. I didn't know quite how important it was until I told them I was going to leave the school. The most important thing they wanted to know was 'who's going to run the chess club now?'.

How valuable are school trips?

When children are nine or ten, primary schools often offer the chance to go away for an activity or educational week, staying away from home. Children benefit from these a great deal; for many it is the highlight of their life at primary school. Many children jump at the chance, some need more encouragement, but it is nearly always worth it. It often brings out a side of children, or skills, that no-one knew they had.

LOOK OUT FOR:

✔ a well-planned trip to places the teachers have visited

✔ a range of activities that are appropriate to your child's age

✔ a safe schedule, with trained staff, especially if there are outdoor pursuits

✔ a mixture of learning and enjoyment

> ### A word of warning
>
> Children have so many opportunities that they can end up doing far too many things. And often parents encourage this – ballet and music on Mondays, pottery and Brownies on Tuesday and so on. Be careful that your child doesn't do too much. Children need to learn to make choices, often between two things they really like. Too much rushing around is not good for you, for them, or for family life. Children need time to be at home and be on their own – to relax and to reflect.

Most activities (apart from most school clubs) cost money. And it can all add up. If money is an issue, especially on schemes run by local councils or school residential trips, you may be eligible for a place at reduced cost. Don't be shy about asking.

Above all, let your child enjoy being a child. This means both learning and hard work, fun and relaxation. Too much of the former may make your child academic but limited, too much of the latter will not help release your child's potential. Good luck and good learning!

Glossary

Attention deficit and hyperactivity disorder (ADHD) A medical condition, diagnosed by a doctor, where children cannot concentrate. Usually associated with disruptive behaviour, more specific than 'being a naughty boy', and more common in boys than girls.

Bullying Bullying is common among children. It is different from arguments or fights. It can include name calling (often about family, race or looks), teasing, ganging up or hurting other children.

Decoding Working out someone else's thoughts from written words (the key skill in reading).

Deep learning The learning about patterns and generalisations which helps us to apply our learning in other situations.

Emergent writing An approach to learning to write based on children's knowledge about print, encouraging them to 'have a go' rather than concentrating on accurate copying.

Encoding Putting your thoughts down into words (the key skill in writing).

English as an additional language The term used where a child's first language is not English.

Extra-curricular activities Clubs in lunchtimes or after school for extra activities such as sports, music or creative arts.

Information and Communications Technology (I.C.T.) The term to replace I.T. (Information Technology) meaning the use of computers and other electronic means to enhance learning.

Key Stages Stages at which a child's education can be assessed, after following a Programme of Study. There are four Key Stages, dividing ages 5-7, 7-11, 11-14 and 14-16.

Literacy Hour The time each day which schools have to devote to teaching literacy skills.

National Curriculum The government's system of education broken into four Key Stages, which applies to all pupils of compulsory school age in maintained schools. It contains core and foundation (non-core) subjects, and incorporates National Tests at the end of each Key Stage.

National Tests Formerly known as SATs these tests are taken in school at the end of each Key Stage – at ages 7, 11 and 14 – to determine what Attainment Target pupils have reached. The scores are also used, especially at age 11, to compare the results of schools as a whole.

Phonics Teaching or learning based on the sounds of letters.

Quality time A time when a child has the full attention of an adult, usually a parent.

Surface learning Learning of facts and content.

USEFUL INFORMATION

Advisory Centre for Education (ACE)
Department A, Unit 1B Aberdeen Studios,
22 Highbury Grove, London N5 2DQ
Web:www.ace-ed.org.uk/
Phone: 020 7354 8321
Free advice, information and support for parents
of children in state schools.

Basic Skills Agency
7th Floor, Commonwealth House,
1-19 New Oxford Street, London WC1A 1NU
Web: www.basic-skills.co.uk/
Phone: 20 7405 4017
National development agency for basic literacy
and numeracy skills.

British Dyslexia Association
98 London Road,
Reading RG1 5AU
Web: www.bda-dyslexia.org.uk
Phone: 0118 966 8271
Fax: 0118 935 1927
Email: info@dyselxiahelp -bda.demon.co.uk
Provides information on dyslexia and access to
local support groups.

DfEE (Department for Education and Employment)
Sanctuary Buildings, Great Smith Street,
London SW1P 3BT
Web: www.dfee.gov.uk
Phone: 020 7925 5555
Free publications on special education can be
sent out, available by phoning 01787 880 946.
Their website on special educational needs is
www.dfee.gov.uk/sen/

National Association for Able Children in Education (NACE)
Westminster College, Oxford OX2 9AT
Web: www.ox-west.ac.uk/nace
Phone: 01865 245 657

National Association for Gifted Children
Elder House, Milton Keynes MK9 1LR
Web: www.rmplc.co.uk/orgs/nagc
Phone: 01908 673 677
Fax: 01908 673 679
Email: nagc@rmplc.co.uk
Provides support groups for counselling for
parents and children. Branches throughout UK.
Information leaflets available.

**National Association for Special
Educational Needs**
NASEN House, 4/5 Amber Business Village,
Amber Close, Amington, Tamworth B774RP
Web: www.nasen.org.uk
Phone: 01827 311 500

**National Confederation for Parent
Teacher Associations (NCPTA)**
2 Ebbsfleet Estate, Stonebridge Road
Gravesend, Kent DA11 9DZ
Web: www.rmplc.co.uk/orgs/ncpta
Phone: 01474 560 618
Promotes partnership between home and
school, children, parents, teachers and education
authorities.

REACH (The National Research Centre for
Children with Reading Difficulties)
California Country Park, Nine Mile Ride,
Finshampstead, Berkshire RG40 4HT
Phone: 0118 973 7575
Fax: 0118 973 7105
Web: www.reach-reading.demon.co.uk
For anyone caring for a child with a disability,
illness or learning problem which affects their
reading, language or communication.

WEBSITES

www.hometown.aol.com/wiseowlsw
A UK children.s specialist in education software
to play online or download.

www.bbc.co.uk/education/schools/
primary.shtml
Home and school learning resources for
children. The BBC education site as a whole has
resources to cover a large range of educational
issues.